Part 1:
Learning Letters

Trace the letters and practice writing them in the remaining space!

Use the blank practice page to write on your own at the end.

A B C D E F G H I J K L M N O P Q R S T U V W X Y Z

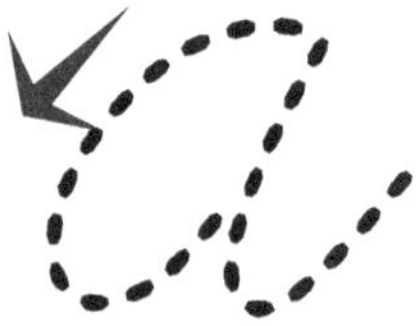

a a a a a a a a a a a

a a a a a a a a a a a

A A A A A A A

A A A A A A A

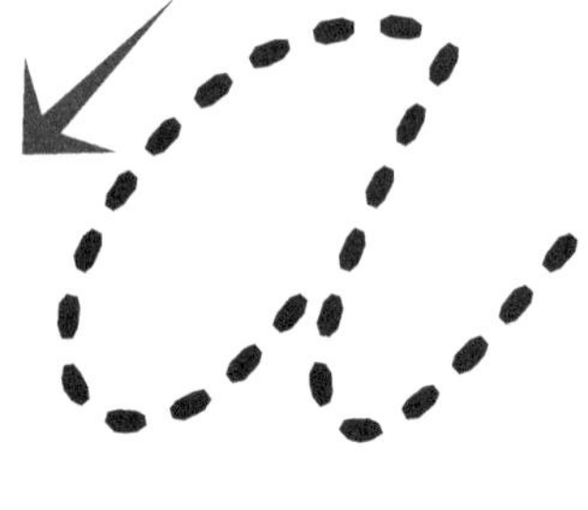

A B C D E F G H I J K L M N O P Q R S T U V W X Y Z

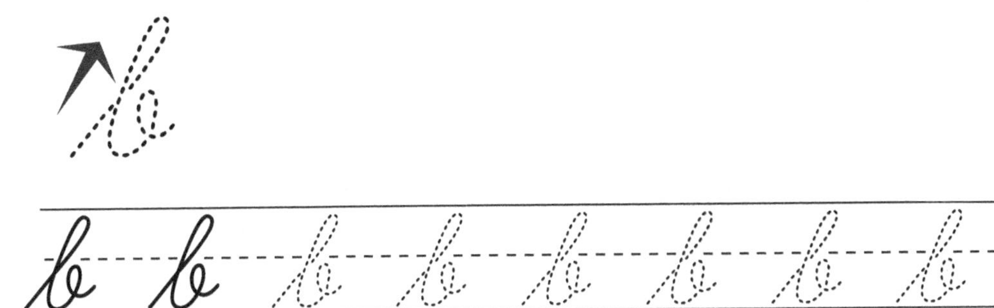

ABCDEFGHIJKLMNOPQRSTUVWXYZ

c c c c c c c c c c c c c

C C c c c c c c c

ABCDEFGHIJKLMNOPQRSTUVWXYZ

A B C D E F G H I J K L M N O P Q R S T U V W X Y Z

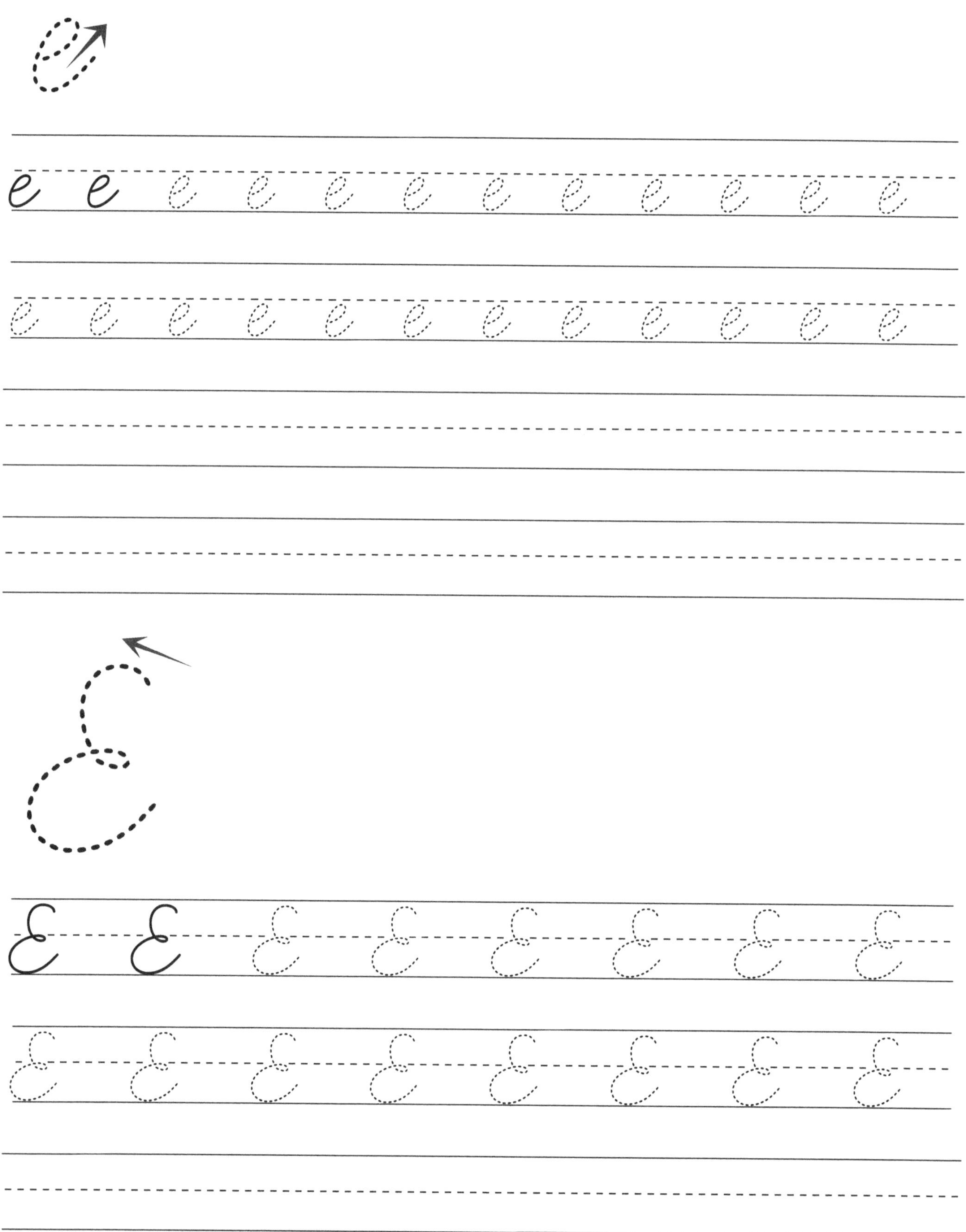

A B C D E F G H I J K L M N O P Q R S T U V W X Y Z

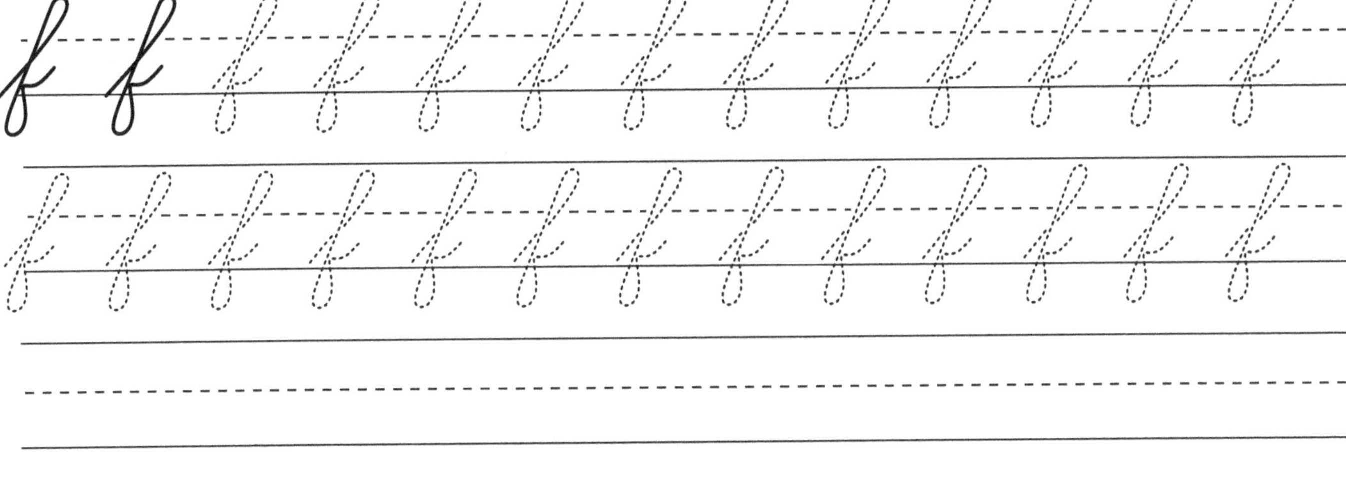

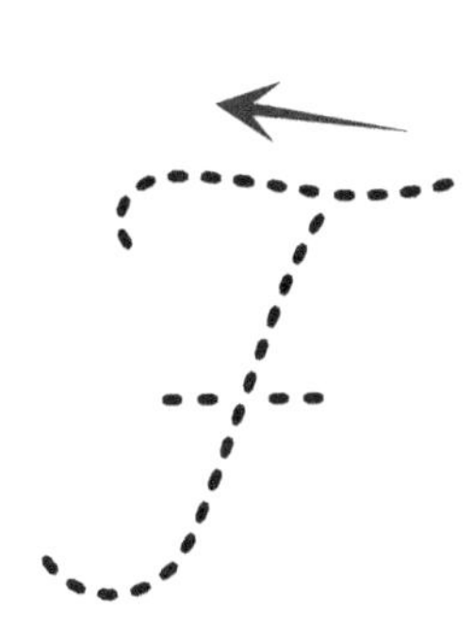

ABCDEF**G**HIJKLMNOPQRSTUVWXYZ

ABCDEFG H IJKLMNOPQRSTUVWXYZ

A B C D E F G H I J K L M N O P Q R S T U V W X Y Z

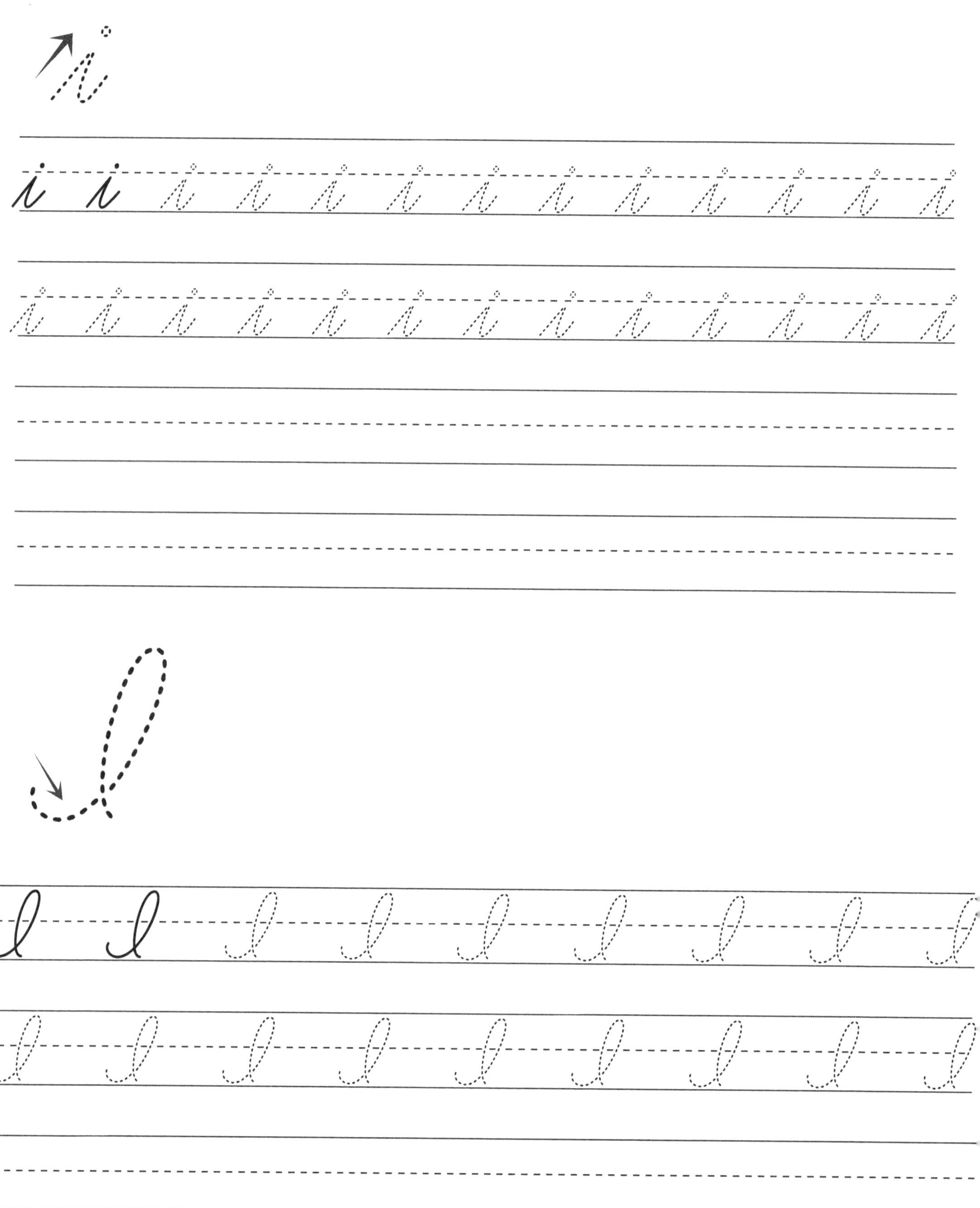

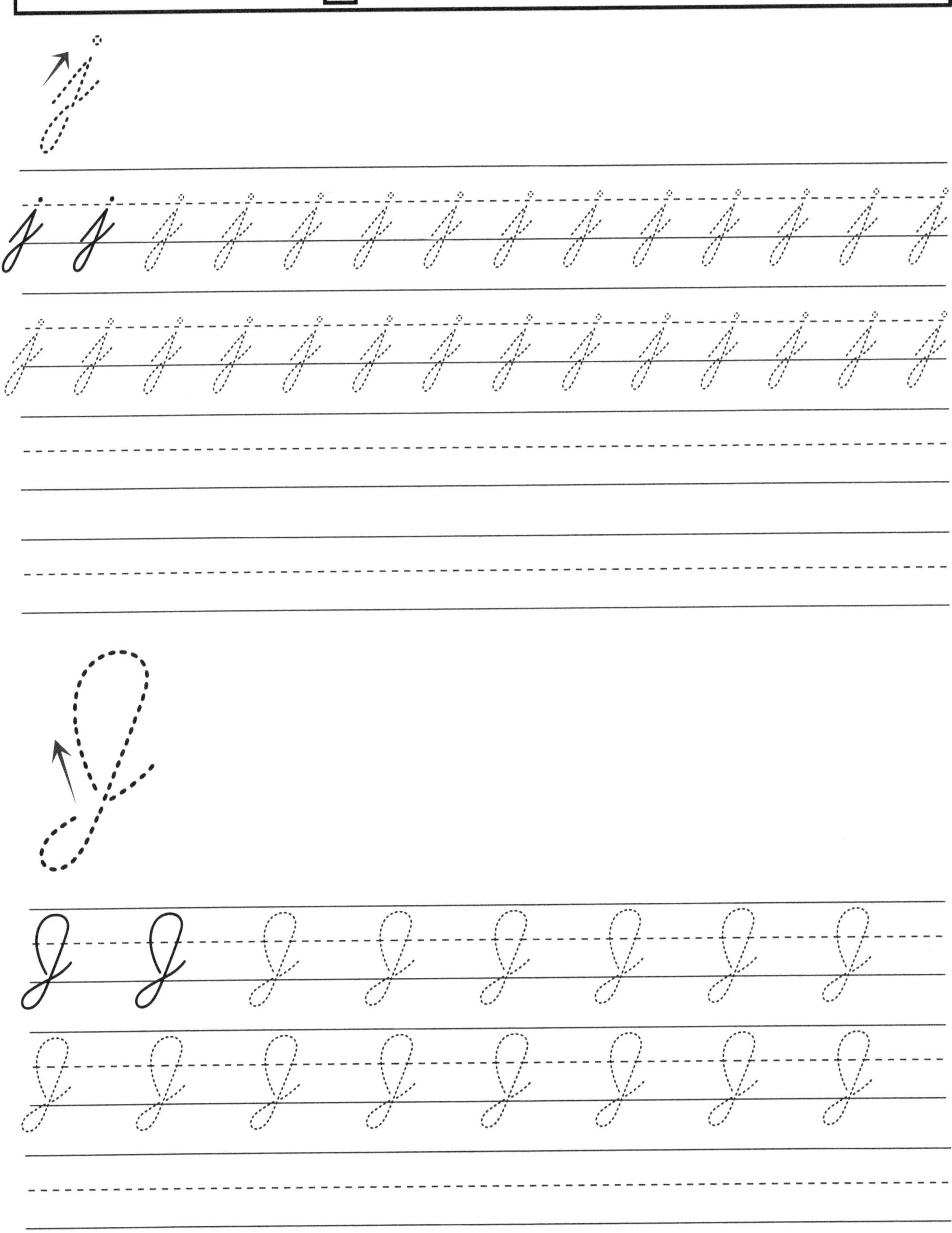

A B C D E F G H I J K L M N O P Q R S T U V W X Y Z

ABCDEFGHIJ**K**LMNOPQRSTUVWXYZ

k k k k k k k k k k k k

k k k k k k k k k k k k

K K K K K K K K

K K K K K K K K

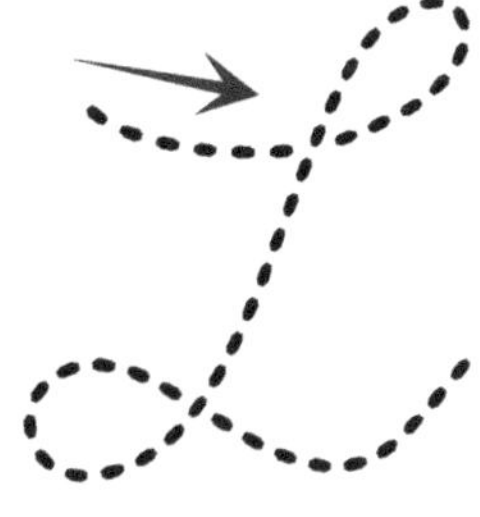

ABCDEFGHIJKL**M**NOPQRSTUVWXYZ

ABCDEFGHIJKLMN O PQRSTUVWXYZ

A B C D E F G H I J K L M N O P Q R S T U V W X Y Z

ABCDEFGHIJKLMNOP[Q]RSTUVWXYZ

A B C D E F G H I J K L M N O P Q R S T U V W X Y Z

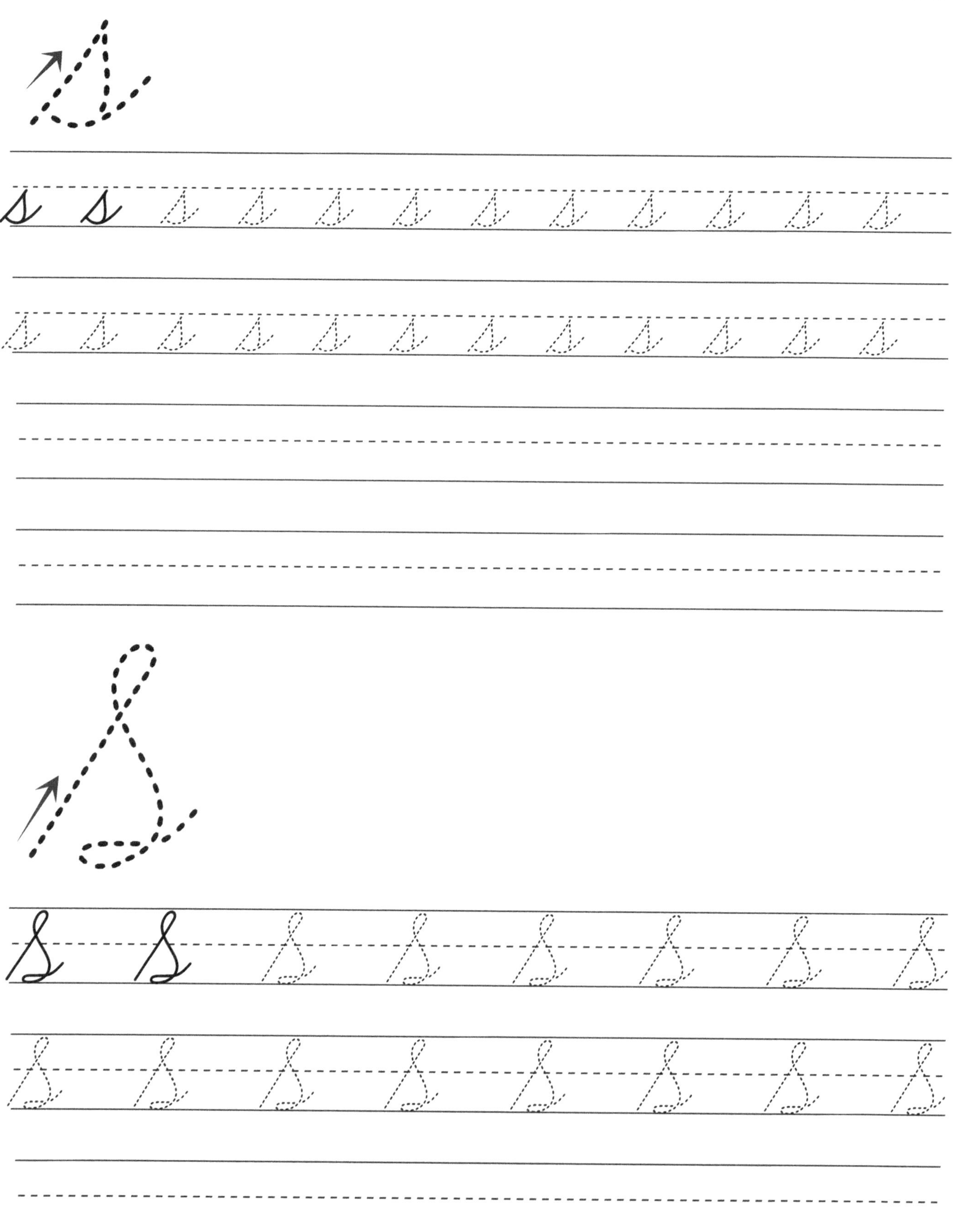

A B C D E F G H I J K L M N O P Q R S T U V W X Y Z

A B C D E F G H I J K L M N O P Q R S [T] U V W X Y Z

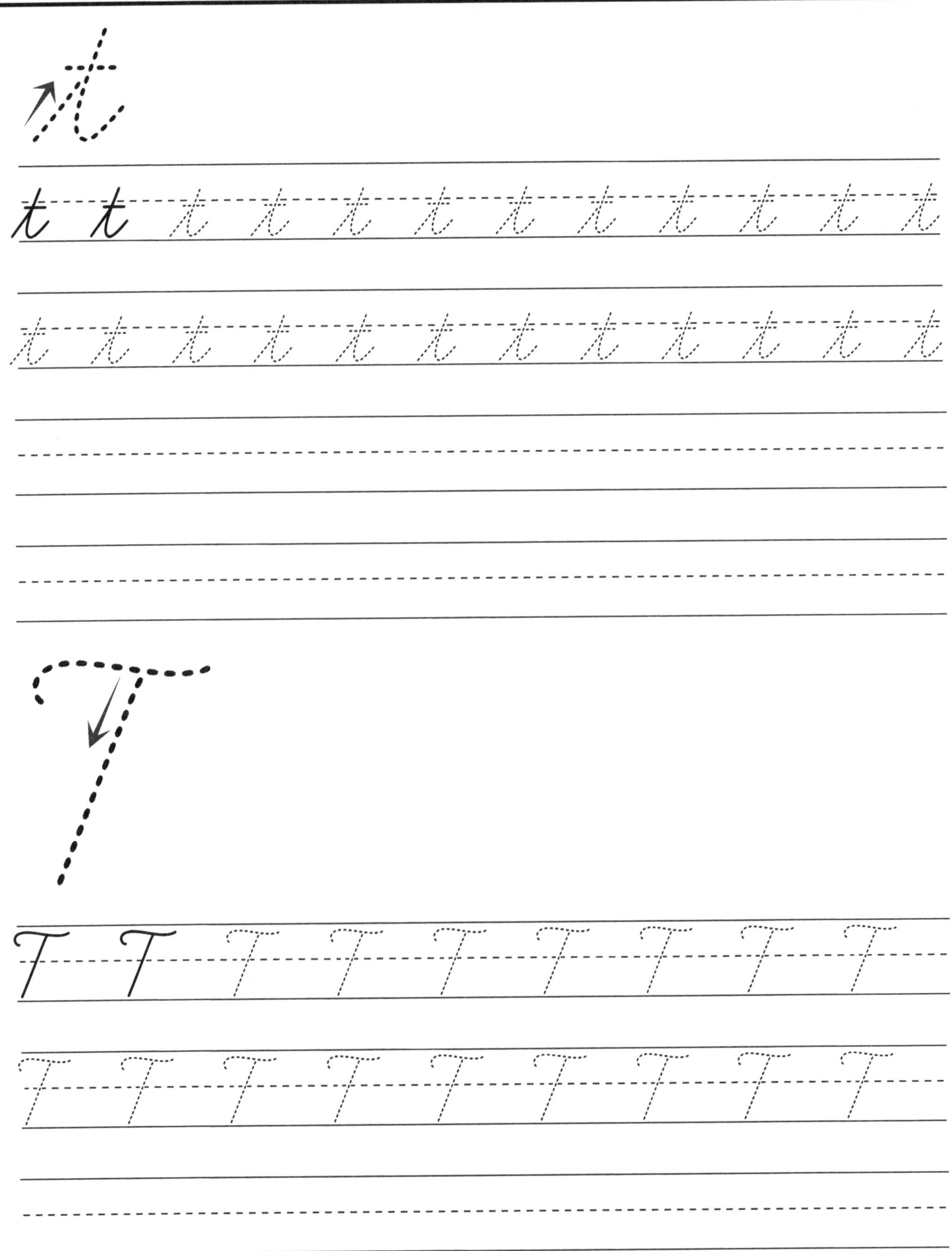

ABCDEFGHIJKLMNOPQRST U VWXYZ

A B C D E F G H I J K L M N O P Q R S T U V W X Y Z

A B C D E F G H I J K L M N O P Q R S T U V W X Y Z

ABCDEFGHIJKLMNOPQRSTUVW X YZ

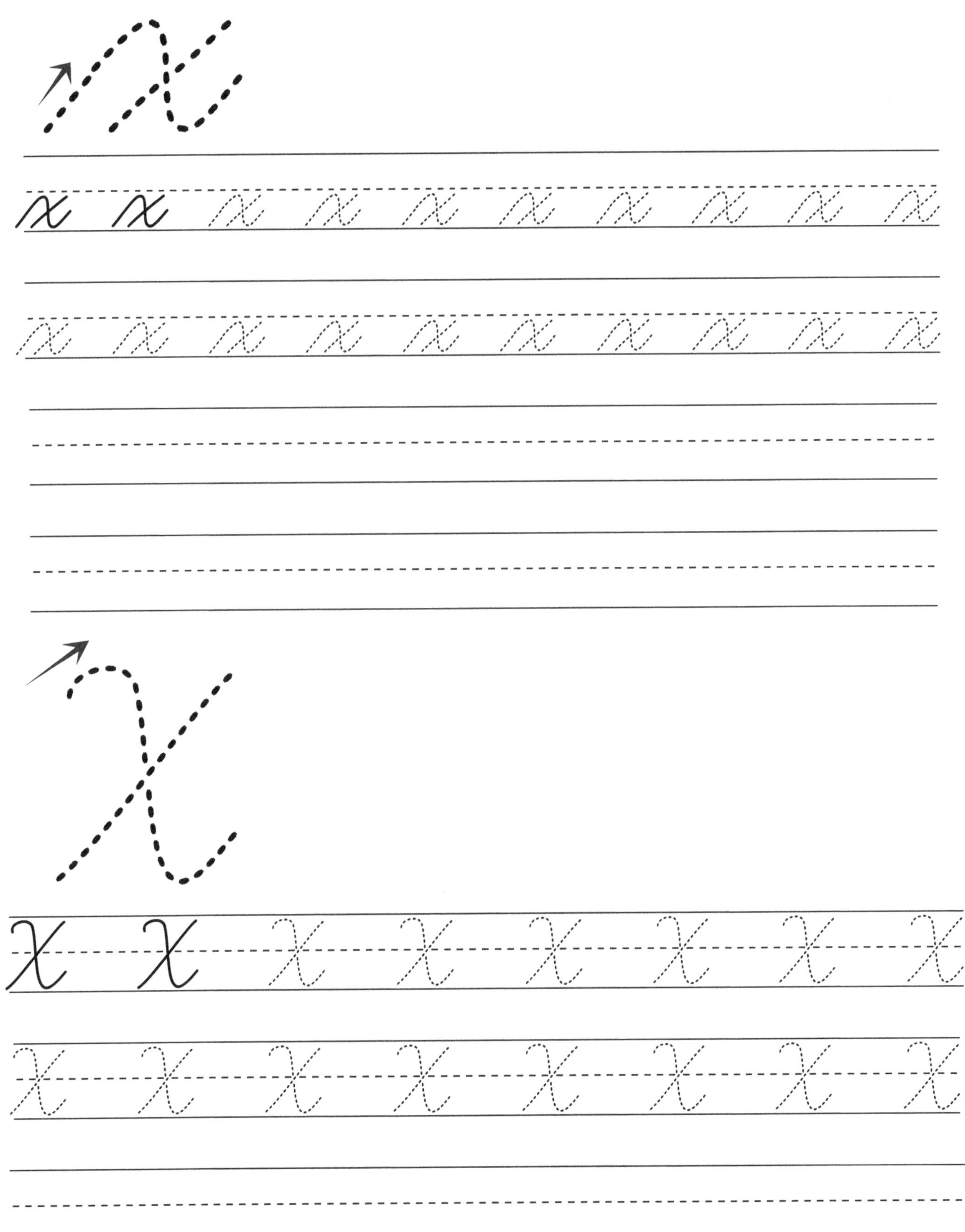

A B C D E F G H I J K L M N O P Q R S T U V W X Y Z

ABCDEFGHIJKLMNOPQRSTUVWXYZ

Part 2: Learning Words

Trace the words and practice writing them in the remaining space!

Use the blank practice page to write on your own at the end.

boy *boy* *boy* *boy* *boy*

girl *girl* *girl* *girl* *girl*

boy and girl

baby *baby* *baby* *baby*

kids *kids* *kids* *kids* *kids*

baby kids

great *great* *great* *great*

food *food* *food* *food* *food*

great food

truck truck truck truck

car car car car car car

truck and car

cute *cute* *cute* *cute* *cute*

fun *fun* *fun* *fun* *fun*

nice *nice* *nice* *nice* *nice*

candy *candy* *candy*

mom *mom* *mom* *mom*

dady *dady* *dady* *dady*

mom and dady

best best best best best

good good good good

best and good

what   what   what   what

who   who   who   who

what and who

each each each each each

tree tree tree tree tree

each and tree

farm *farm* *farm* *farm*

sky *sky* *sky* *sky* *sky*

farm and sky

lunch *lunch* *lunch* *lunch*

dinner *dinner* *dinner*

lunch and dinner

class   class   class   class

family   family   family

class and family

ground   *ground*   *ground*

heard   *heard*   *heard*   *heard*

ground and heard

guice   *guice*   *guice*   *guice*

merry   *merry*   *merry*

guice and merry

orange *orange* *orange*

apple *apple* *apple* *apple*

orange and apple

Picture Picture Picture

Queen Queen Queen Queen

picture and queen

Running   Running

Shield   Shield   Shield

running and shield

Teacher Teacher Teacher

Student Student Student

teacher and student

Brother *Brother* *Brother*

Sister *Sister* *Sister* *Sister*

brother and sister

Part 3: Learning Numbers

Trace the numbers and practice writing them in the remaining space!

Use the blank practice page to write on your own at the end.

1 1 1 1 1 1 1 1 1 1

1 1 1 1 1 1 1 1 1 1

One One One One

One One One One

2 2 2 2 2 2 2 2

2 2 2 2 2 2 2 2

Two Two Two Two

Two Two Two Two

3 3 3 3 3 3 3 3

3 3 3 3 3 3 3 3

Three Three Three Three

Three Three Three Three

4   4   4   4   4   4   4   4

4   4   4   4   4   4   4   4

Four   Four   Four   Four

Four   Four   Four   Four

5 5 5 5 5 5 5 5

5 5 5 5 5 5 5 5

Five Five Five Five

Five Five Five Five

7 7 7 7 7 7 7 7

7 7 7 7 7 7 7 7

Seven Seven Seven

Seven Seven Seven

8 8 8 8 8 8 8 8

8 8 8 8 8 8 8 8

Eight Eight Eight

Eight Eight Eight

9 9 9 9 9 9 9 9

9 9 9 9 9 9 9 9

Nine Nine Nine

Nine Nine Nine

10   10   10   10   10   10

10   10   10   10   10   10

Ten   Ten   Ten   Ten   Ten

Ten   Ten   Ten   Ten   Ten

GREAT
You did it!

Alligator

Bear

Cat

Duck

Elephant

Flamingo

G
Giraffe

Horse

I

Iguana

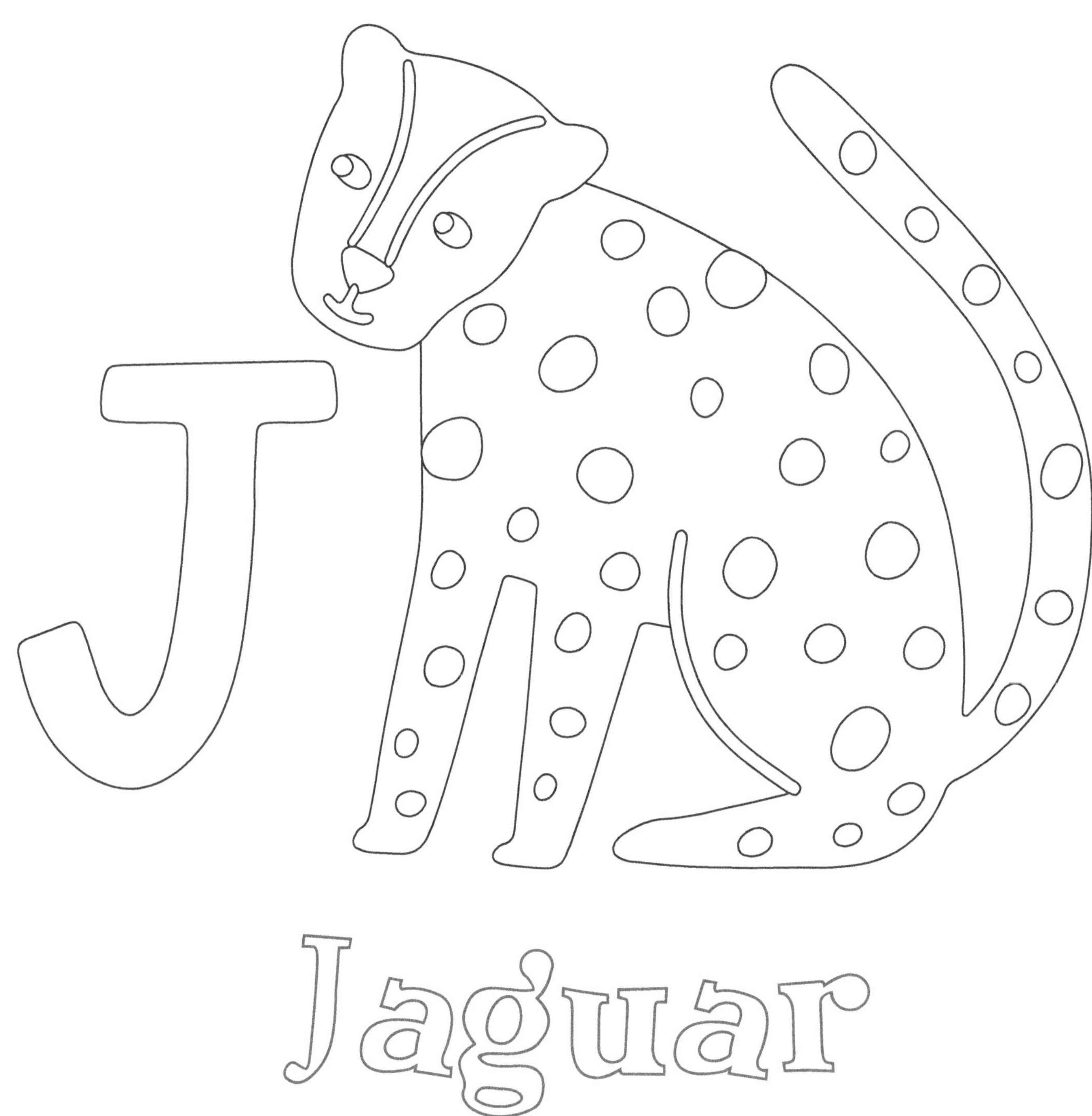

J
Jaguar

Koala

L
Lama

Monkey

N

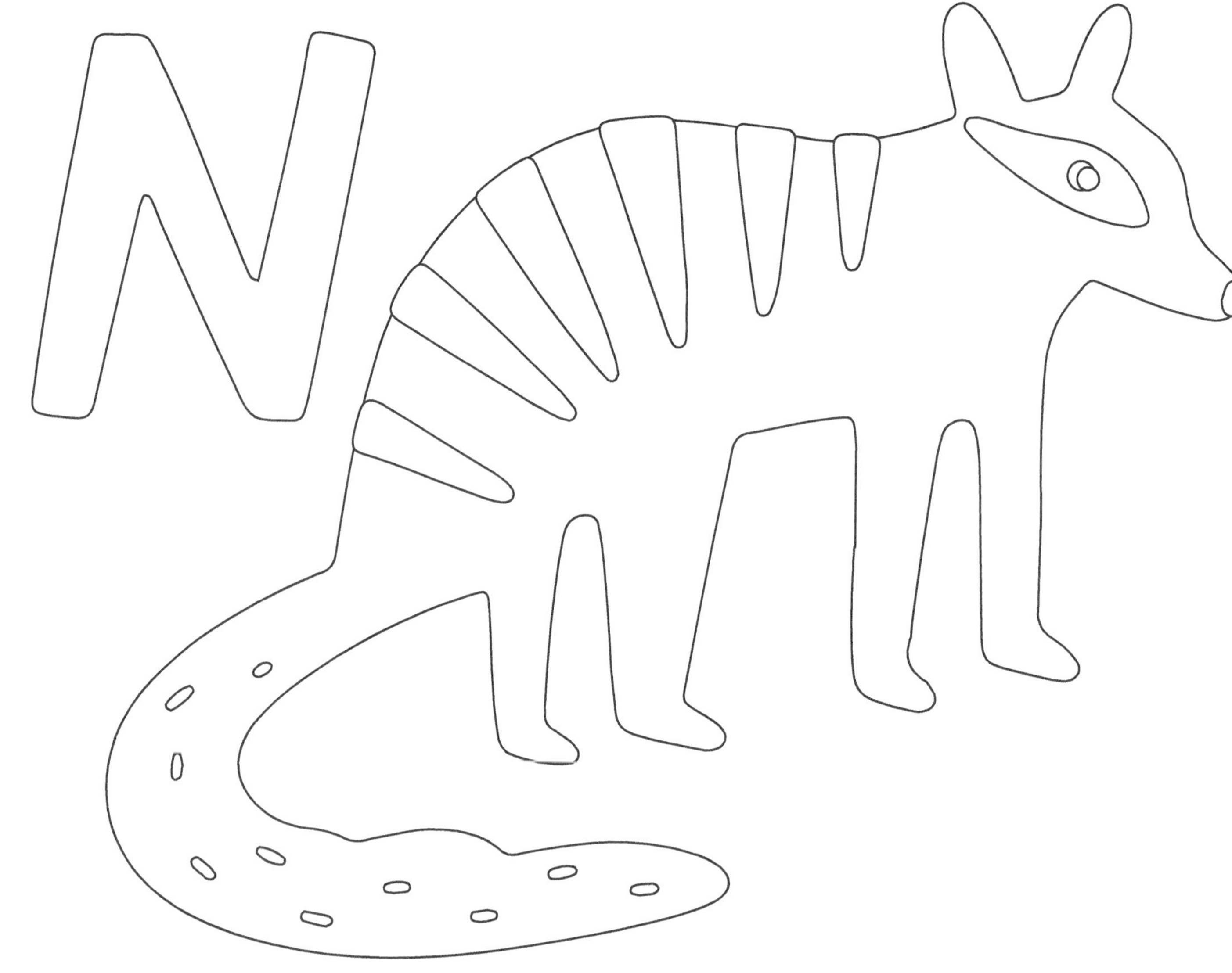

Numbat

O
Owl

Penguin

Q
Quail

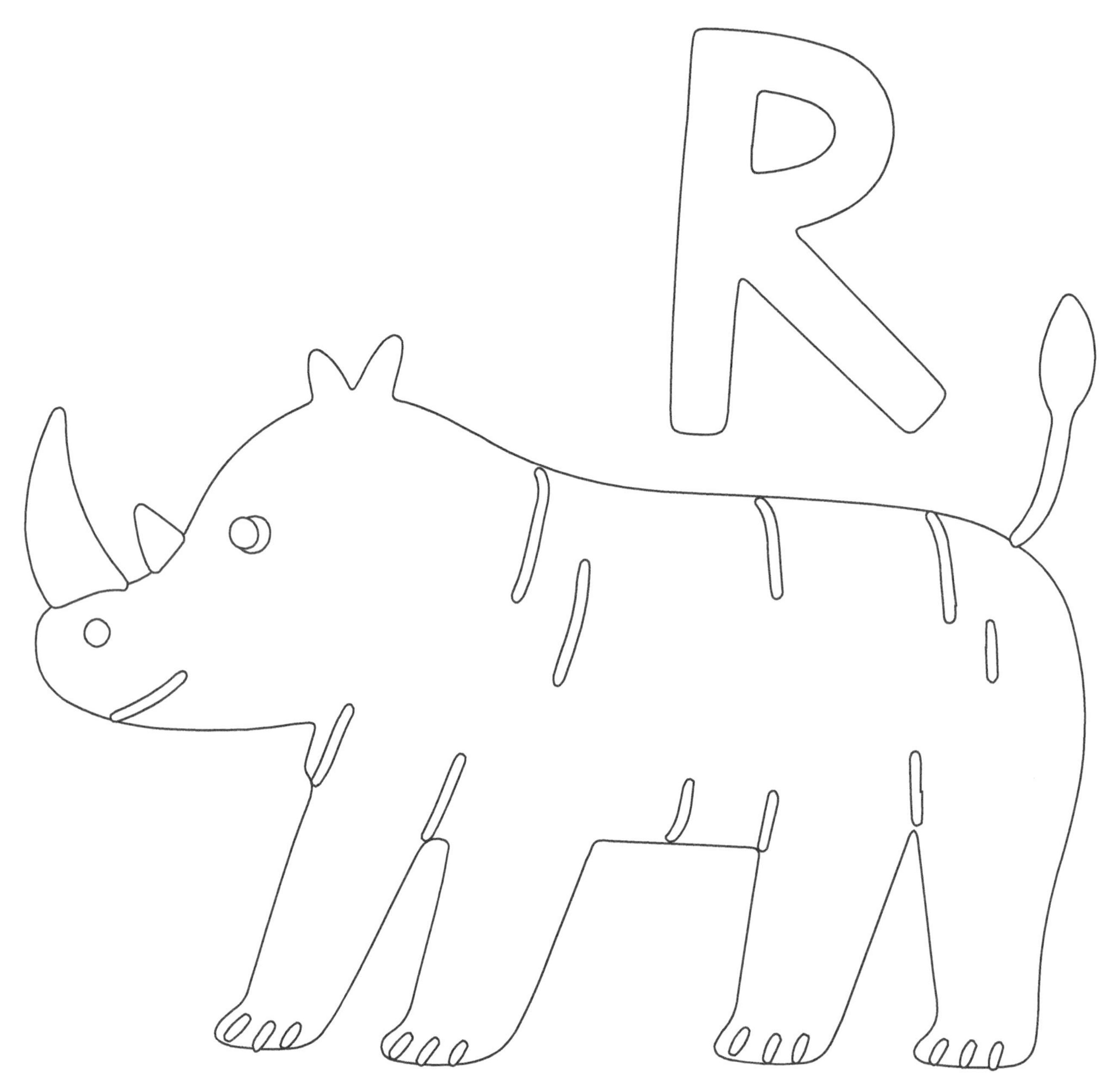

R
Rhinoceros

S
Sheep

Tiger

Unicorn

V
Vampire
Bat

Whale

Xerus

Yak

Z
Zebra